CORE LIBRARY OF US STATES

OKLAHOMA

BY LYNN TERNUS
CONTENT CONSULTANT
Erin Brown
Collections Specialist
Oklahoma Territorial Museum & Historic Carnegie Library

Core Library

An Imprint of Abdo Publishing
abdobooks.com

abdobooks.com

Published by Abdo Publishing, a division of ABDO, PO Box 398166, Minneapolis, Minnesota 55439. Copyright © 2023 by Abdo Consulting Group, Inc. International copyrights reserved in all countries. No part of this book may be reproduced in any form without written permission from the publisher. Core Library™ is a trademark and logo of Abdo Publishing.

Printed in the United States of America, North Mankato, Minnesota.
052022
092022

Cover Photo: Shutterstock Images, map and icons, Oklahoma City
Interior Photos: Greg Nelson/Sports Illustrated/Getty Images, 4–5; Red Line Editorial, 7 (Oklahoma), 7 (USA); iStockphoto, 9, 17, 22–23, 43; Prisma/Universal Images Group/Getty Images, 12–13; Lukasz Stefanski/Shutterstock Images, 15 (flag); Shutterstock Images, 15 (bison), 15 (rose); Natalia Kuzmina/Shutterstock Images, 15 (bird); Peter Haynes/iStockphoto, 15 (tree); Eugene R. Thieszen/Shutterstock Images, 25; Nattapong Assalee/Shutterstock Images, 27; Bob Pool/Shutterstock Images, 30–31, 45; Alizada Studios/Shutterstock Images, 33; J Pat Carter/Getty Images News/Getty Images, 36–37; Patrick Horton/Shutterstock Images, 41

Editor: Angela Lim
Series Designer: Joshua Olson

Library of Congress Control Number: 2021951572

Publisher's Cataloging-in-Publication Data

Names: Ternus, Lynn, author.
Title: Oklahoma / by Lynn Ternus
Description: Minneapolis, Minnesota : Abdo Publishing, 2023 | Series: Core library of US states | Includes online resources and index.
Identifiers: ISBN 9781532197772 (lib. bdg.) | ISBN 9781098270537 (ebook)
Subjects: LCSH: U.S. states--Juvenile literature. | Southwestern States--Juvenile literature. | Oklahoma--History--Juvenile literature. | Physical geography--United States--Juvenile literature.
Classification: DDC 976.6--dc23

Population demographics broken down by race and ethnicity come from the 2019 census estimate. Population totals come from the 2020 census.

CONTENTS

CHAPTER ONE
The Sooner State **4**

CHAPTER TWO
History of Oklahoma **12**

CHAPTER THREE
Geography and Climate **22**

CHAPTER FOUR
Resources and Economy **30**

CHAPTER FIVE
People and Places **36**

Important Dates 42

Stop and Think 44

Glossary 46

Online Resources 47

Learn More 47

Index 48

About the Author 48

CHAPTER ONE

THE SOONER STATE

A crowd of fans and students erupts into roars and cheers as the Sooners enter the Oklahoma Memorial Stadium. They are ready for Saturday night college football at the University of Oklahoma in Norman. Tonight is a big game. The Sooners are taking on their biggest rival, the Texas Longhorns. The marching band begins playing "Boomer Sooner," the university's fight song. Oklahoma fans dress in

The University of Oklahoma cheerleaders took the field before a game against West Virginia in 2017.

THE FIRST SOONERS

On March 23, 1889, President Benjamin Harrison signed a document. This would open a section of Oklahoma's lands for settlers. Beginning April 22 of that year, people arriving in the region could claim up to 160 acres (65 ha) of land as their own. This led to a rush of people entering Oklahoma. Some of them came to the area before the appointed starting time. These people were called Sooners. Many people admired the Sooners for their hard work and can-do attitudes. In the early 1900s, Oklahoma took on this term as its state nickname.

crimson and shout out the lyrics as the time to kickoff nears.

Since 1908 the University of Oklahoma's football team has been known as the Sooners. The term was first used to describe early US settlers to the region. Today Oklahoma's nickname, the Sooner State, is a form of state pride.

ABOUT OKLAHOMA

Oklahoma borders six states. Colorado and Kansas make its northern border. Missouri and Arkansas

MAP OF OKLAHOMA

This map of Oklahoma shows some of the major landmarks and cities in the state. Why do you think Oklahoma City is in the middle of the state? What's significant about its location?

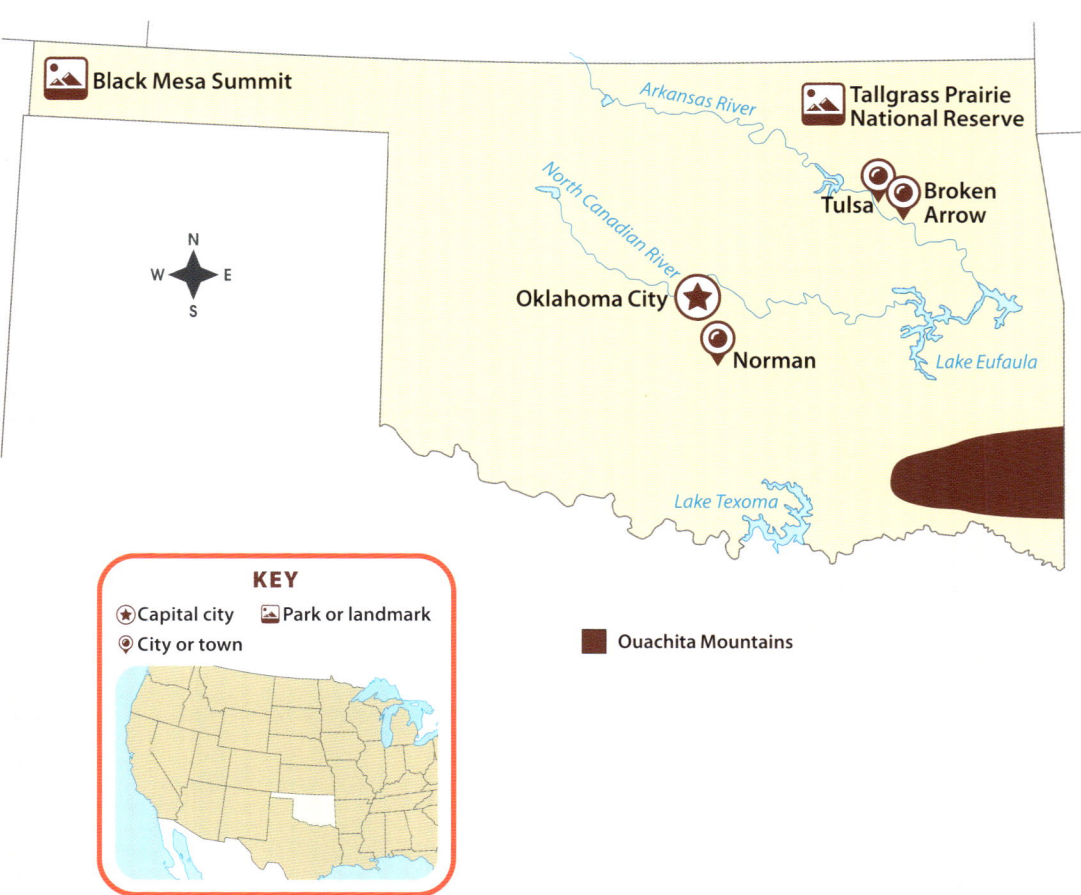

are to the east. Texas is south of Oklahoma. One of Oklahoma's defining features is its Panhandle region, a narrow strip of land that looks like the handle of a pan. New Mexico borders this region to the west.

Oklahoma is part of the South. The state shares culture with other southern states, especially in cuisine. For example, Oklahomans enjoy traditionally southern foods, such as catfish and hushpuppies. But the state's culture and geography are varied. Parts of the state grow large amounts of wheat, making it similar to midwestern states. Canyons and mountains lie in the southwestern part of the state. This region has many similarities with the Southwest. Because of the regional diversity, some Oklahomans see their state as a blend of cultures.

A diverse group of people also call Oklahoma home. This includes American Indian nations such as the Cherokee Nation and the Choctaw Nation. It also includes Black and Hispanic Americans.

Oklahoma City has been the state capital since 1910.

Many people live in Oklahoma City, the largest city in the state. It has a population of more than 680,000. Oklahoma City is also the state's capital. It is located in the central part of the state. It sits beside the North Canadian River.

Approximately 100 miles (161 km) northeast of the state capital is Oklahoma's second-largest city, Tulsa. The city lies along the Arkansas River. Other cities in

PERSPECTIVES

TULSA REMOTE

Tulsa Remote is a program that encourages remote workers to move to Tulsa, Oklahoma. Remote workers are able to work from home. They don't need to travel to an office or other location to do their jobs. Tulsa Remote offers $10,000 to move to the city. Housing is cheaper in Tulsa than in many other US cities. The city has other benefits too, such as a tight-knit community. Alana Mbanza moved to the city as part of Tulsa Remote. She said, "Two months into moving to Tulsa, I had enough friends to host a Super Bowl party."

Oklahoma include Norman, in the central region of the state, and Broken Arrow, in the northeast.

Farming is an important industry for the state. Oklahoma is also a major producer of oil and natural gas. But Oklahoma is more than what the land provides. Big cities offer shops, sports arenas, and more. Rural areas offer beautiful parks for people looking for outdoor adventures. Oklahoma is an exciting state to explore.

STRAIGHT TO THE
SOURCE

In February 2020 Lieutenant Governor Matt Pinnell revealed his work to rebrand Oklahoma. He wanted the rest of the nation to be aware that the state could be a popular tourist destination. He described the process in a speech:

> *Last summer I invited more than 200 of Oklahoma's brightest and most creative . . . to join me in creating a new brand for Oklahoma. Their task was to develop a cohesive, new brand for Oklahoma that best represents our heritage and history, our booming industry, our beautiful one of a kind vistas, and most importantly, our greatest asset—our people. The vision behind this effort is to position Oklahoma as a top-tier destination for visitors, businesses, talent and citizens.*
>
> Source: "Oklahoma's New Brand and Logo Unveiled." *Oklahoma Commerce*, 12 Feb. 2020, okcommerce.gov. Accessed 12 May 2021.

BACK IT UP

The speaker is using evidence to support a point. Write a paragraph describing the point the speaker is making. Then write down two or three pieces of evidence the speaker uses to make the point.

CHAPTER TWO

HISTORY OF OKLAHOMA

Historians estimate that people have lived in Oklahoma for 30,000 years. They have found evidence of these early peoples from historic sites throughout the state. They continue to study how these peoples arrived in the region.

Over time these cultures continued to change. Approximately 2,000 years ago, they started to build more permanent settlements and relied more on agriculture. Modern American Indian nations including the Wichita,

This depiction of the 1889 Land Rush shows settlers arriving at Main Street in Purcell, Oklahoma.

Caddo, and Wahzhazhe (Osage) came from these early cultures.

Other American Indian nations arrived in the region in the 1500s. They included the Kiowa, who moved from plains in Canada. The arrival of these nations created conflicts with American Indian nations already living in the area.

AMERICAN INDIAN NATIONS

Spanish explorers first arrived in the Oklahoma area in the 1500s. They came in search of gold. They also forced American Indian peoples in the region to convert to Christianity.

French explorers came to the region in the 1600s. They claimed the area for France. The French traded with some American Indian nations, such as the Wichita. The French exchanged guns and cloth for furs.

But European explorers also brought new diseases with them. Contact with these explorers caused

OKLAHOMA
QUICK FACTS

Each US state has its own unique culture and history. Take a close look at the state symbols of Oklahoma. What do they show you about the history of the state?

Abbreviation: OK
Nickname: The Sooner State
Motto: *Labor omnia vincit* (Work conquers all things)
Date of statehood: November 16, 1907
Capital: Oklahoma City
Population: 3,959,353
Area: 69,899 square miles (181,038 sq km)

STATE SYMBOLS

State animal
American bison

State flower
Oklahoma rose

State bird
Scissor-tailed flycatcher

State tree
Redbud

15

American Indian peoples to become sick. Many died from smallpox and measles.

In 1803 the US government purchased a large area of land from France. This was called the Louisiana Purchase. The new land included what is now Oklahoma.

The US Congress passed the Indian Removal Act in 1830. The act allowed the US government to force American Indian peoples out of their homelands and into Oklahoma. US settlers were interested in the southeastern land that belonged to American Indian nations. The Muscogee (Creek), Choctaw, and Cherokee peoples had all lived in Georgia for thousands of years. Their long journey to Oklahoma became known as the Trail of Tears. As much as 25 percent of the Cherokee people died on the Trail of Tears. Over several decades the US government moved more American Indian nations into Oklahoma.

US settlers rushed to Oklahoma to claim farmland during the 1889 Land Rush.

WHITE SETTLERS MOVE IN

Some American Indian nations in Oklahoma sided with the Confederacy during the American Civil War (1861–1865). The Confederacy tried to separate from the United States in order to keep slavery legal. Nations that joined the Confederacy did so for multiple reasons. Some practiced slavery. Many were unhappy with the US government, which had pushed them out of their homelands. Some of these nations did not have the resources to remain neutral. The Confederate government worked to ally with these nations whereas the US government showed little interest. In addition, early Confederate victories convinced some nations to join the Confederacy.

The US Army defeated the Confederate Army in 1865. American Indian nations that had sided with the Confederacy had to sign new treaties with the US government. They had to give up large amounts of their land due to their role in the war. The land that had previously belonged to these American Indian nations became known as the Unassigned Lands.

In 1889 the US government made the Unassigned Lands available for settlement. People rushed to Oklahoma to claim land. Oklahoma became a territory in 1890. The discovery of oil in the late 1890s and early 1900s brought even more people to the region.

Settlers in the Oklahoma Territory wanted the region to become a US state. However, some lawmakers did not want to accept the territory as an individual state. In 1906 President Theodore Roosevelt combined the Oklahoma Territory with the surrounding Indian Territory. Oklahoma became the forty-sixth US state on November 16, 1907.

OKLAHOMA IN THE 1900s

During the 1900s Black people faced discrimination from white people. In Oklahoma and other parts of the United States, segregation kept people of color separate from white people. Oftentimes these separate facilities were not equal to what white people had. Race relations became tense, sometimes leading to violence and riots.

During the Great Depression (1929–1939) many people in Oklahoma and throughout the United States lost their homes. Farmers in Oklahoma struggled

THE TULSA RACE MASSACRE

The Greenwood District in Tulsa was a predominantly Black neighborhood. In 1921 Tulsa police arrested a Black man named Dick Rowland. Newspaper reporters claimed he had attacked a white woman, but the arrest was made without an investigation. White people stormed the Greenwood District, destroying homes and businesses. As many as 300 people, many of whom were Black, died in the event known as the Tulsa Race Massacre.

because of a severe drought. In addition, high winds blew dry soil around, creating dust storms. The area became known as the Dust Bowl. Many Oklahomans left their homes to find jobs in other states.

PERSPECTIVES
LIFE DURING THE DUST BOWL
In the early 1900s, farmers began developing large areas of the Great Plains for farmland. This destroyed the grasses that held down the soil. Droughts and high winds in the 1930s also contributed to the Dust Bowl. J. R. Davison lived in Oklahoma during this time. He recalled an instance when he saw a dust storm rolling in. He said, "We could see this low cloud bank. . . . And we watched that thing and it got closer. . . . The ends of it would seem to sweep around. And you felt like, you know, you were surrounded. Finally, it'd just close in on you, shut off all light."

GOVERNMENT
Oklahoma has three branches of government. The legislative, executive, and judicial branches have different responsibilities. Legislative officials create and vote on new bills. The executive branch includes a governor,

who can sign bills into laws. The judicial branch includes the Oklahoma courts, such as the Supreme Court of Oklahoma.

Today there are 39 federally recognized tribes in Oklahoma. Some of these nations have lived in the region for thousands of years. Others were forced to move to the area as a result of the Indian Removal Act. Each tribe has its own unique system of government with elected officials.

FURTHER EVIDENCE

Chapter Two talks about American Indian land. Identify one main point made about the American Indian peoples living in Oklahoma. What evidence does the author provide to support this point? Read the article at the website below. Does the information on the website support the main point of the chapter? Does it present new evidence?

SUPREME COURT RULES THAT ABOUT HALF OF OKLAHOMA IS NATIVE AMERICAN LAND

abdocorelibrary.com/oklahoma

CHAPTER
THREE

GEOGRAPHY AND CLIMATE

Oklahoma has many landscapes. The Ouachita Mountains extend from Arkansas into the southeastern part of Oklahoma. This mountain range is one of only a few in the United States that run east to west. Eastern Oklahoma is heavily forested. Oak forests grow in the Wichita Mountains. Visitors today can drive through the Ouachita National Forest and enjoy scenic views amidst the trees. The Ozark Plateau in the northeast is another forested region in the state.

The Wichita Mountains are located in southwestern Oklahoma.

The landscape flattens into prairies in the central part of the state. It includes meadows and plains that make good farmland. This region is known as the Osage Plains. Settlers used the land for agriculture. Less than 4 percent of the original prairies remain today. But some of the natural prairie grasses are protected in the Tallgrass Prairie National Preserve. This is the largest prairie preserve in the world.

Grasslands in western Oklahoma are dry and treeless. The plains there are a higher elevation than the central part of the state. Black Mesa Summit, Oklahoma's highest peak, is in the Panhandle region. It stands at 4,973 feet (1,516 m).

Weather varies depending on the landscape and elevation. Oklahoma's eastern region gets more rain than the west. The flat Panhandle region receives approximately 17 inches (43 cm) of rain each year.

Oklahoma belongs to a region that is nicknamed Tornado Alley. Tornadoes are more likely in this

In 2019 Oklahoma set the US record for most tornadoes in a year with 146.

region than in other areas of the United States. The state also experiences thunderstorms. Blizzards are another extreme weather event. They may occur during Oklahoma winters and are more common in the Panhandle region.

Temperatures around the world are rising due to climate change. This is the change in weather patterns over time. Periods of drought are more common. Droughts harm grasslands and crops. Climate change also causes extreme rain events, which increase the risk of floods. In 2019 severe thunderstorms caused flooding of the Arkansas River. More than 2,400 people had to leave their homes. Events like these may become more common in Oklahoma because of climate change.

PERSPECTIVES

SURVIVING A TORNADO

In 2013 a tornado hit Moore, Oklahoma. Homes lay ruined, trees were destroyed, and cars had been flung far. Twenty-four people died in the natural disaster. Sam Riojas survived the tornado. He recalled what his hometown looked like afterward. He said, "Shock is probably the closest descriptive word. It looks like a war zone. . . . People are just in a state, they're just frantic."

PLANT AND ANIMAL LIFE

Different types of plants and animals live throughout Oklahoma. The Ouachita National Forest has many hickory trees and pines. Deer, river otters, and black bears live in this forest. Western

A large population of prairie chickens call the Tallgrass Prairie National Preserve home.

grasslands are drier and host different types of animals. Burrowing frogs, prairie dogs, and meadowlarks can all be found in the region.

American bison were once common in Oklahoma's western plains. They are an important part of many American Indian cultures in the region, including the Kiowa. Approximately 30 million bison roamed the

EASTERN COLLARED LIZARD

The eastern collared lizard is Oklahoma's state lizard. The male lizard has a blue or green body. The female is brown to gray. Both the male and the female have yellow or orange markings. The bright colors attract mates. A black collar rings the lizard's neck. The eastern collared lizard is also called the mountain boomer. It lives in rocky habitats. The lizard is most active during the day. It needs Oklahoma's sunny climate to stay warm. Insects make up most of the lizard's diet.

Great Plains in the 1400s. But overhunting by European and American settlers sharply reduced the bison population. By the late 1800s, fewer than 1,000 of these animals remained. Today people work to protect these creatures. People can see bison in the Tallgrass Prairie National Preserve and other wildlife areas throughout the state.

The Tallgrass Prairie National Preserve is home to many types of wildlife. Visitors can see more than 300 types of birds, including the scissor-tailed flycatcher.

The bird is named for its long, forked tail. It is Oklahoma's state bird.

The soil in some parts of Oklahoma is fertile and good for gardening and growing crops. The Oklahoma rose is a popular choice among gardeners. These dark-red, sweetly scented roses are the state flower. The pink blossoms of redbud trees are another attractive choice for landscaping. Redbuds are the state trees of Oklahoma. They are native to the region.

EXPLORE ONLINE

Chapter Three discusses the effects of climate change on Oklahoma's wildlife. The article at the website below goes into more depth on climate change's impact on Oklahoma's birds. After reading the information, what did you learn about climate change and birds living in the state?

HOW CLIMATE CHANGE WILL AFFECT OKLAHOMA'S BIRDS

abdocorelibrary.com/oklahoma

CHAPTER FOUR

RESOURCES AND ECONOMY

Agriculture is an important part of Oklahoma's economy. Much of the agricultural industry in the state today is focused on livestock and wheat production. Oklahoma is the second-largest producer of beef in the United States. It's also known for other livestock, such as poultry and swine. Oklahoma is the fourth-largest grower of wheat. The state also produces cotton and soybeans.

Oklahoma's cattle industry brings in more than $2 billion to the state each year.

POWER SOURCES

Much of Oklahoma's economy comes from the energy sector. The land in Oklahoma is rich in fossil fuels such as oil and natural gas. Oil was first discovered in the region in 1897. The industry experienced severe declines in the 1980s.

Oklahoma's oil industry began growing again around the 2000s. Today fossil fuels continue to play an important role in the state's economy. In 2020 the state was the fourth-largest producer of both oil and natural gas in the country.

PERSPECTIVES

RANCHING IN OKLAHOMA

Vikki Schumacher is a fourth-generation rancher. She and her husband, John, own a cattle ranch in Boise City, Oklahoma. Vikki's family, including her daughter and son-in-law, look after approximately 13,000 cows on the ranch. "Day-to-day working on a ranch is fun. I enjoy it, just [to] get out in the open air and get to see God's work," said Vikki. "Cattle ranching is very important to us. We want to carry on the legacy of what we have known all of our lives."

The Devon Oil and Gas Exploration Park is located in Oklahoma City.

Fracking is the process of using water pressure and chemicals to break up rocks deep underground. It is a way to access more fossil fuels. Oklahoma companies use fracking to get natural gas. But fracking can have serious consequences. Fracking causes earthquakes in Oklahoma. Fracking can also poison groundwater.

Oklahoma also uses renewable energy. By 2019 the state was getting more than 30 percent of its electricity from renewable energy sources, such as wind. Oklahoma ranked third in the nation in wind energy in 2020.

OTHER IMPORTANT INDUSTRIES

Fuels are not the state's only natural resources. Mining occurs in all 77 Oklahoma counties. Gypsum and salt

VISITING OKLAHOMA LAKES

Oklahoma has more than 200 human-made lakes, the most of any US state. People built dams for many reasons, including flood control and hydropower. The dams created lakes. Lake Texoma and Lake Eufaula are two of the state's largest lakes. They are the results of dams and are popular tourist destinations. People enjoy running along sandy beaches and boating across the lakes.

are two important minerals in the state. Companies can use minerals to make chemical products such as chlorine, which is used for cleaning.

Tourism is the third-largest industry in Oklahoma. In 2018 approximately 21.5 million people visited the state. They spent $9.6 billion. The state government promotes all the activities people can do in Oklahoma. Visitors to Oklahoma's 35 state parks can enjoy scenic views, hiking trails, and campsites. The cities are bursting with local restaurants, festivals, and art.

STRAIGHT TO THE SOURCE

Many people debate about the future of energy. Some people want to keep using fossil fuels, while others hope to turn to renewable sources. Reporter Jack Money notes that talks concerning energy resources have been going on for years:

> *Debates about ways to support the energy industry . . . have been part of every presidential and congressional election since the 1980s, and . . . governmental actions have prompted applause or angst as they have helped or hurt energy production along the way. . . .*
>
> *While the number of Oklahomans employed by oil and gas companies in the state is relatively small, the industry's impact on the overall health of the state's economy . . . is huge.*
>
> Source: Jack Money. "Biden's Administration Could Affect Oklahoma's Energy Industry in Surprising Ways." *USA Today*, 18 Jan. 2021, usatoday.com. Accessed 1 Apr. 2021.

WHAT'S THE BIG IDEA?

Take a close look at this passage. What is the main point Money makes about the energy industry? Find two or three details used to support that main point.

36

CHAPTER
FIVE

PEOPLE AND PLACES

Around 3.9 million people lived in Oklahoma in 2019, with 75 percent of the population being non-Hispanic white. Hispanic or Latino people make up approximately 11 percent of the population. American Indians make up 9.4 percent of the population. Some American Indians live on reservations located throughout the state. Black people make up 7.8 percent of people living in Oklahoma.

Children from the Cheyenne and Arapaho Tribes celebrated their culture during the Red Earth Native American Festival parade in 2016.

37

PERSPECTIVES
FIGHT FOR EQUALITY

Ada Lois Sipuel Fisher wanted to go to law school at the University of Oklahoma in 1946. The university rejected her application because she was Black. Fisher fought for her right to attend law school. Her case ultimately went to the US Supreme Court. It ruled that Fisher must have equal education opportunities compared to her white peers. She was admitted to the University of Oklahoma law school in 1949. Her court case helped end segregation in public schools nationwide.

Several famous figures are from Oklahoma. Actor Brad Pitt was born in Shawnee. Wide receiver Tyler Lockett plays for the National Football League and grew up in Tulsa. Author Ralph Ellison hailed from Oklahoma City. He won the 1953 National Book Award for his novel *Invisible Man.* Many famous country singers were also born in Oklahoma, including Blake Shelton, Carrie Underwood, Reba McEntire, Toby Keith, and Garth Brooks. Additionally, several famous American Indian authors grew up or live in Oklahoma. Joy Harjo is a poet and member of the Muscogee Nation. In 2019 she became the first American Indian Poet Laureate of the United States. The Poet Laureate works to promote poetry in the country.

American Indian cultures are a large part of the state's rich heritage. Annual public gatherings highlight the unique American Indian cultures in Oklahoma today. For instance, the Red Earth Festival takes place each year in Oklahoma City. More than 1,000 American

HISPANIC CULTURES

For the early part of the state's history, the majority of Oklahoma's Hispanic population had Mexican roots. Today people of Mexican heritage celebrate cultural holidays such as Mexican Independence Day on September 16. Oklahoma's Hispanic population has grown to include large communities of people with Puerto Rican, Cuban, and Guatemalan backgrounds. The Hispanic population is the fastest-growing racial group in the state. Hispanic people celebrate their unique cultures and work to have their voices heard in politics and media.

Indian dancers and artists from more than 100 nations and tribes attend.

La Fiesta de Tulsa is another cultural festival in Oklahoma. People celebrate Latin American cultures through music, dance, and art. They can also enjoy cuisines from Latin American countries.

IMPORTANT PLACES

Big cities bring in big crowds for sporting events. Norman is home to the University of Oklahoma and the Sooners sports teams. During the 2018–2019 basketball season, the Oklahoma City Thunder recorded sellout games. People in Oklahoma City can also enjoy concerts, theater, art museums, and botanical gardens.

Those interested in the outdoors can explore Oklahoma's many landscapes. Alabaster Caverns is the largest alabaster cave open to the public. Alabaster is a form of the mineral gypsum. It is usually white, but the cave has rare black alabaster. Visitors can hike through the cave and see bats. Natural Falls State Park is in

Scenes from the 1974 film *Where the Red Fern Grows* were filmed at Natural Falls State Park.

eastern Oklahoma. The waterfall is 77 feet (23 m) tall. People can camp nearby and look at wildlife. From big cities to natural getaways, Oklahoma has activities for everyone to enjoy.

IMPORTANT DATES

30,000 years ago
The first people arrive in Oklahoma.

1500s CE
Kiowa and other American Indian nations arrive in the Oklahoma region. Spanish explorers travel through the area in search of gold.

1600s
French traders enter the region and trade with American Indian nations.

1830
Congress passes the Indian Removal Act. American Indian nations such as the Muscogee, Choctaw, and Cherokee are forced to move to Oklahoma.

1889
President Benjamin Harrison signs a document to open the Unassigned Lands to white settlers on March 23. This leads to a rush of people arriving in present-day Oklahoma.

1890
Oklahoma becomes a US territory.

1907
Oklahoma becomes the forty-sixth US state on November 16.

1921
White rioters destroy Black-owned homes and businesses during the Tulsa Race Massacre. As many as 300 people die in the violence.

2019
Severe thunderstorms and flooding of the Arkansas River cause many Oklahomans to leave their homes.

STOP AND THINK

Say What?

Studying US states can mean learning a lot of new vocabulary. Find five words in this book you've never heard before. Use a dictionary to find out what they mean. Then write the meanings in your own words and use each word in a new sentence.

Take a Stand

Fracking is a part of Oklahoma's energy industry. But it can harm the environment. Do you think fracking should continue in Oklahoma? Why or why not?

Another View

This book talks about mining. As you know, every source is different. Ask a librarian or another adult to help you find another source about this practice. Write a short essay comparing and contrasting the new source's point of view with that of this book's author. What is the point of view of each author? How are they similar and why? How are they different and why?

You Are There

This book discusses Oklahoma's landscapes. Imagine you are hiking through the Great Plains. Write a letter home telling your friends about the experience. What plants and animals do you see? Be sure to add plenty of detail to your notes.

GLOSSARY

depression
a period of time when the economy struggles, usually causing job loss

discrimination
when people treat others differently based on certain factors such as appearance

elevation
the height above sea level

heritage
cultural history or background that is passed down through families and communities

massacre
the act of killing many people who are usually helpless or innocent

reservation
an area of land set aside for American Indian people

territory
an area of land that is not a state but is still controlled by a country

treaty
an official agreement between governments

ONLINE RESOURCES

To learn more about Oklahoma, visit our free resource websites below.

Core Library CONNECTION
FREE! COMMON CORE MULTIMEDIA RESOURCES

Visit **abdocorelibrary.com** or scan this QR code for free Common Core resources for teachers and students, including vetted activities, multimedia, and booklinks, for deeper subject comprehension.

Booklinks NONFICTION NETWORK
FREE! ONLINE NONFICTION RESOURCES

Visit **abdobooklinks.com** or scan this QR code for free additional online weblinks for further learning. These links are routinely monitored and updated to provide the most current information available.

LEARN MORE

Harris, Duchess, and A. R. Carser. *The Tulsa Race Riot*. Abdo, 2020.

Ryan, Todd. *Oklahoma Sooners*. Abdo, 2021.

INDEX

agriculture, 13, 24, 31
American Indians, 8, 13–14, 16–18, 21, 27, 37–39
Arkansas River, 7, 9, 26

bison, 15, 27–28
Black Americans, 8, 19, 37, 38
Black Mesa Summit, 7, 24

diseases, 14
drought, 20, 26
Dust Bowl, 20

eastern collared lizard, 28
explorers, 14

fracking, 33

geography, 8, 23–24
government, 16–18, 20–21, 34, 35

Harjo, Joy, 38–39
Hispanic Americans, 8, 37, 39, 40

Indian Removal Act, 16, 21

Louisiana Purchase, 16

mining, 33–34

Oklahoma City, 7, 9, 15, 38–40

Ouachita National Forest, 23, 26

Panhandle, 8, 24–25
Pinnell, Matt, 11

segregation, 18, 38
settlers, 6, 13, 16–18, 24, 28
Sooners, 5–6, 15, 40

Tallgrass Prairie National Preserve, 7, 24, 28–29
Tornado Alley, 24
tornadoes, 24, 26
tourism, 11, 34

About the Author

Lynn Ternus is a children's book writer who lives in northern Minnesota.